Autobiography of Death

Also by Kim Hyesoon

All the Garbage of the World, Unite!
I'm OK, I'm Pig!
Mommy Must Be a Fountain of Feathers
Poor Love Machine
Sorrowtoothpaste Mirrorcream
When the Plug Gets Unplugged
Princess Abandoned
Anxiety of Words: Contemporary Poetry by Korean Women: Ch'oe Sŭng-ja,
      Kim Hyesoon, Yi Yŏn-ju

Autobiography of Death

Kim Hyesoon

Drawings by Fi Jae Lee

Translated from the Korean by Don Mee Choi

 A New Directions Paperbook Original

The publication of this book was supported by a grant from the Literature Translation Institute of Korea (LTI Korea).

LTI Korea
Literature Translation Institute of Korea

Manufactured in the United States of America
First published as a New Directions Paperbook (NDP1429) in 2018
Design by Marian Bantjes

Library of Congress Cataloging-in-Publication Data
Names: Kim, Hye-sun, 1955– author. | Choi, Don Mee, translator.
Title: Autobiography of death / Kim Hyesoon ; drawings by Fi Jae Lee ; translated by Don Mee Choi.
Description: New York : New Directions, 2018.
Identifiers: LCCN 2018021515 (print) | LCCN 2018025538 (ebook) | ISBN 9780811227353 (ebook) | ISBN 9780811227346 (alk. paper)
Subjects: LCSH: Kim, Hye-sun, 1955– —Translations into English.
Classification: LCC PL992.415.H886 (ebook) | LCC PL992.415.H886 A2 2018 (print) | DDC 895.71/4—dc23
LC record available at https://lccn.loc.gov/2018021515

10 9 8 7 6 5

New Directions Books are published for James Laughlin
by New Directions Publishing Corporation
80 Eighth Avenue, New York 10011

Contents

Autobiography of Death

Commute

DAY ONE

On the subway your eyes roll up once. That's eternity.

The rolled-up eyes eternally magnified.

You must have bounced out of the train. It seems that you're dying.

Even though you're dying, you think. Even though you're dying, you listen.

Oh what's wrong with this woman? People. Passing by.
You're a piece of discarded trash. Garbage to be ignored.

As soon as the train leaves, an old man comes over.
He discreetly inserts black fingernails inside your pants.

A moment later he steals your handbag.
Two middle schoolers come over. They rummage around in your pockets.
They kick. Camera shutters click.
Your funeral photo is on the boys' cell phones.

You watch the panorama unfold in front of you like the dead normally do.
Your gaze directed outward now departs for the vast space inside you.

Death is something that storms in from the outside. The universe inside is
        bigger.
It's deep. Soon you float up inside it.

She's stretched out over there. Like a pair of discarded pants.
When you pull up the left leg, the right leg of your pants runs faraway,
        your unsewn clothes, your zipperless clothes swirl around. At the
        corner of the subway of your morning commute.
Pitiful. At one point the woman was embraced as bones clasp marrow,
embraced as bra cups breasts.

Black hair, coming and going, clutches. Your single outfit.

A dinosaur is about to come out of the woman's body.
She opens her eyes wide. But there's no exit left.

The woman's dead. Turned off like the night sun.
Now the woman's spoon can be discarded.
Now the woman's shadow can be folded.
Now the woman's shoes can be removed.

You run away from yourself. Like a bird far from its shadow.
You decide to escape the misfortune of living with that woman.

You shout, I don't have any feeling whatsoever for that woman!
But you roll your eyes the way the woman did when she was alive
and continue on your way to work as before. You go without your body.

Will I get to work on time? You head toward the life you won't be living.

Calendar

DAY TWO

A white rabbit dies and becomes a red rabbit.
It bleeds even after it's dead.
Soon the red rabbit becomes a black rabbit.
It rots even after it's dead.
Because it's dead, it can become big or small at will.
When it's huge, it's like a cloud, and when it's tiny, it's like an ant.
You try shoving an ant rabbit into your ear.
The ant rabbit eats everything in sight, the wide grass field inside your ear,
then it gives birth to two bunnies bigger than a storm cloud.
Your ears are buzzing. Every sound is buzzing. Your ear is dying. A rabbit is
      dying.
Sometimes a dead rabbit reincarnates as a bloodied menstrual pad.
Occasionally you pull out a dead rabbit from your panties.

Every month you pull out a dead rabbit and hang it on the wall.

On the wall you hang a crying that smells like rabbits' ears.

Photograph

DAY THREE

How's your doll?
How's your doll's health?

You speak into your doll's ears, It's a secret! Shut your mouth for life!
As you pluck out your doll's eyes, You liked it too, didn't you? That's it, isn't
    it?
As you cut off your doll's hair, Die you filthy bitch!
As you set your doll on fire, You've forgotten about your past life forever,
    haven't you?

When you leave the house, your doll stays behind
When you leave the house, your doll comes back to life
When you leave the house, your doll opens the window and looks out
When you leave the house, your doll leaves the house
When you leave the house, your doll pretends it's an orphan

That thing, it says it can't eat in front of people for some reason
That thing, it never dies
That empty thing
That thing worships your ghost in its pupils

Doll is walking over there, its armless arms come out then go back in
Its legless legs come out then go back in
like someone who's left her legs behind on her bed

Crumpled paper from its legs scatter

Your doll walks
Your doll talks

Drops its eyes inside itself
Cries till its neck turns all the way around

It may come back to life when you die

Anyhow you can no longer make your doll stand
Anyhow you can no longer make your doll walk
Anyhow you can no longer make your doll laugh

You are now disconnected from your doll

You write a letter

Dear Doll: You still need someone to put you to bed every night and close
    your eyes

Lean on the Water

Lean your body on the water and cling to it

Can't bear it any longer. I twist my body
holding on to the fingers of water and

wear a coat woven with water's hair
I crouch and cover my face

Let's be slant together
Let's fall embracing each other

After I jump off
it'll be your turn to jump

When I throw down the fishing line
please bite on the hook and bob up
I'll do the same next time

Plead to

the water that talks to itself more than you do

It babbles on when it's drunk
so I take the rain home

Water pours in through the window

You're about to lean
on it
but the water
leans on you even more

Midnight Sun

DAY FIVE

A letter arrives from a place where your reply can't be sent

That you're already here
That you've already left you

A shimmering letter arrives from the hole that knows everything

Like the brain that sees all too clearly after death, a bright letter arrives
Like the days before you were born, a widely wide letter without yesterday
      or tomorrow arrives

Soft chiming of bells from a carriage made of light
Giggles of a girl in pants made of light, knocking on the nightless world

The last train runs above ground
the world where all the trains on the platform light up at once and silently
      forget about you

You can't go, for you are footless, but the children of your childhood are
      already there
A letter arrives from that bright hole where not even a reply in black can be
      sent

where your children age in front of you
from that place where you departed to, to be reincarnated

A letter arrives, written in ink of brightly bright light

from that place where you've never encountered darkness
an enormously enormous letter arrives
a brilliant light a newborn greets for the first time

After You're Gone

DAY SIX

After you've gone don't go, don't
After you've come don't come, don't

When you depart, they close your eyes, put your hands together and cry
       don't go, don't go
But when you say open the door, open the door, they say don't come, don't
       come

They glue a paper doll onto a bamboo stick and say don't come, don't come
They throw your clothes into the fire and say don't come, don't come

That's why you're footless
wingless

yet all you do is fly
unable to land

You're visible even when you hide
You know everything even without a brain

You feel so cold
even without a body

That's why this morning the nightgown hiding under the bed
is sobbing quietly to itself

Water collects in your coffin
You've already left the coffin

Your head's imprint on the moon pillow
Your body's imprint on the cloud blanket

So after you've gone don't go, don't
So after you've come don't come, don't

Tibet

Your expression dissipates at night
Your name dissipates at night

You bark *kung kung* at your own name that's running away
like a dog barking at the moon

Now you head out to the open field where only the present unfolds

Hence fatigue is called the nameless horizon!

Anxiety is called the weightless, boundless width!

Misfortune is called the beyond the timberline that no one looks back at!

Fear is called the snowfield where you can catch a glimpse of the
   expressionless Yeti!

Sorrow is called the infinite sky where neither being nor nonbeing exists!

(The universe is teeming with five twin siblings!)

kung
kung
kung
kung
kung

Orphan

DAY EIGHT

Not God, you're a square

You grow up calling death Mommy
You drink death juice, counting the grains of death

You're the square's servant
You're the square's bastard
You're the square's bellboy

A square horse drags you along

Your body is tied up in the four corners forever
When you open your eyes, it always runs toward four directions

God is love, you're farewell
You were born from farewell and die of farewell

(Your face is now wiped transparent with a damp towel)
(Your hands are wiped clear)
(The soul's breathing is in the body) (The body's breathing is in the square)

The TV on the wall, a scene of an eight-nippled mommy pig eating the
        brain of its ninth piglet

A scene of orphan death being born before it dies

Now your body fits perfectly into the square dress

Everyday Everyday Everyday

DAY NINE

You're holding the receiver but you're not here
You're wearing your earbuds but you're not here

The dead girl talks into a toy phone
Can I speak to my mommy? I want to sing a song for her

You're eating but you're not at the table
where maggots feast on my descendants' abdomens

The call's not going through right now but it should be alright by Sunday
      night
Will it really be okay by Saturday morning after Sunday night?

You're here but not here
You're there but not there

What if I get a tattoo on my face?
Then will I be here?

Please give me the there
the arrival after arrival

The lonely child without a phone
The girl's face is as big as the sky, the dark cloud

Like when the boats tickle the inside of your garment
Like when you talk into the mic and confess your love

Like fog, like smoke, the there tomorrow
Here is not the place, now is not the time

Sunlight tickles the heap of trash floating down the river
The tomorrow that escaped from your body turns around to look at you

The there is not there but here
Mommy makes money and will come tomorrow, comes every, every
       tomorrow

The faces of people holding their phones like mirrors inside the packed
       subway
are already there like the evaporated dew drops in the morning

The phone rings there
Your tongue is already there, flapping about like a tropical fish on the mist-
       soaked asphalt

Namesake

You're an older sister. You raise your sister
You have breakfast together sleep together laugh together
You change her clothes and bathe her
At home you're always together
You only go out by yourself
The incoming call punctures your togetherness
We found your sister's body but...
You tell your sister that her body has been found
Yet you still live together, you dream and make friends on her behalf
Even after you identify your sister's body
you have dreams about her sinking in the sea
You eat together sleep together watch TV together
You feel most at ease living with your sister

When you stand by the sea, something, a black lump falls from the sky

Butterfly

This is the way to know that you're already dead

Blow onto the window
Put your hand on the left side of your chest

They say birth is always a plunge
and death is always a flight
so take off from the cliff's edge

Are you the daily plunge toward the paper's surface? Or are you the flight?
A butterfly standing on one leg dips its other leg into red ink and writes a
         letter

Mommy: You can't start laughing as soon as you're born?
You: No, I'm just seeing if I can!

When the plunge begins the flight of the scream also begins
The center of the abyss rises infinitely
Your wings flutter like ripples on the water
Now are you liberated from yourself?

Your feet have no prints
Your happiness has no breaths
Your letter has no name

You're as white as the salt in tears
You're as ah ah ah ah as the wind's yawn

Are you now vertigo without privacy?

Now you've become so light that you won't be able to plunge at all
You're merely a ripple upon ripple of the top floor of the abyss

Lunar Eclipse
DAY TWELVE

A black, plump bird, as big as you, was at the door. You got up and took off your nightgown and put on a black outfit. You had a hunch that you were about to receive a message. You were skinny, but the bird was chubby. In real life, or perhaps in your dream, you heard a knocking at the window. You opened the window, but there was no one. You only saw something trying to stand up, like a shadow flittering in the wind, something that had lived stuck to the ground its entire life. As you opened the door and stepped into the convenience store, something tugged at your ankle. A hand came up swiftly like a burp from a dark pit. You heard a familiar voice: Let's go, let's go to the unknown place, deepest place, bottom of the bottom. You were afraid that an unknown face might appear in the toilet water, in the mirror. You wondered whether terror comes before sorrow. You shouted into the receiver, Don't bother calling if you're not going to come! There was someone listening at the other end. Once there was a lunar eclipse and, at the moment of the full eclipse, the doors of the wardrobe opened wide then someone crawled out saying: Let's go let's go. Startled, you screamed, and cold energy embraced you. The 24-hour movie theater had gone bust, yet you felt as if you were standing in the middle of a field where films show non-stop, and your father called the funeral parlor and requested a coffin made of limestone instead of wood. That way water won't get in, bugs won't get in, so it'll stay nice and dry, Father said. You were sitting at the dining table, but you couldn't feel your body as if you'd stepped out of a film. Even though you chewed loudly, none of it felt real. What more can I eat? When you turned around, there was nothing on the table.

Do you want to be a friendly corpse?
Do you want to be a scary corpse?

Do you want to become silk that ghosts kiss?
Do you want to become a sack that ghosts kick?

Every, every day is the eve of death

The orator strikes his palm down on the table

Gravel Skirt

1. *Garden of Fingers*

You're a rock
No one can touch you
You have a gravel skirt on,
you're at the temple of ruins
You're lying on a rock bed

Your poor garden
Your shitty garden
Your garden extends from your ten fingers
Your garden stinks of gravel

I'll scream
I'll beg
The garden where your dress breaks, your face breaks

The moon is terrifying because it's faraway
A terrifying island floats around the dark sky
When it comes too near, pebbles drip down on the moon's cheeks plop plop

We raised the moon long ago, remember?
The moon used to scramble onto our bed and burrow between us
When we took a stroll
with the moon strung around our wrist
your skirt went up in flames, yellowy, willowy

Yet tonight
The sick moon, its broken face lies in the garden
When you touch it, the moon's fingers drip down plop plop

In the shitty garden, the moon breaks alone

2. *Heart's Seashore*

Your heart dies like pebbles by the riverbank

Your heart dies like the sandy shore

Your breathing stops like the dark moon

Behind you, the days that couldn't become you sob and break like waves

Nest

DAY FOURTEEN

Eyebrows: Two maggots trace strands of rain as they move

Ears: Turn your head slightly and suck up the insides through a straw

Smile: A sip of foul breath suspended momentarily in the air
      (Can I float here forever?)
      (Can I watch from up here?)

Eyes: Two sips of sea jelly, it's very salty

Toenails: I carefully planted ten seeds

Knees: Newborn twins stick their faces out

(I'm being shoved out of the only body I have in the world)

(When the door of the upright face opens
the screams of the night sky pour down like a waterfall)

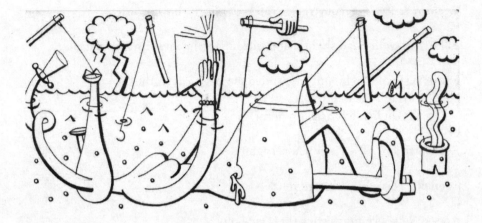

Death's Magic-Compressed Distance

DAY FIFTEEN

If I'd known it'd be like this, I'd have given my piddly breasts to the orphan
If I'd known it'd be like this, I'd have given my piddly eyes to the fish
If I'd known it'd be like this, I'd have given my piddly head to the rose

In the room, the woman gasps
(At the windowsill her hair is blowing)
(Her tongue fits into the keyhole)
(Her womb turns on the light brightly)

Woman, you're dead
Water your shadow and your grave blooms
Grave of shame, guilt, insult

Woman, you're dead
Open your heart's door and the crimson grains quickly disperse
Red blood cells of fatigue, melancholy, fear

Woman, you're dead
You're a doll
You're a mule
You're a pony with pierced nostrils

The woman gasps. As her lips part, her shy skull's teeth line up like dining
room chairs. As her yellowish flesh hardens, her shy red roses turn blue. Put
a mask on that woman's rose! The prison door opens and her rancid-smelling
heart is laid out. Put a diaper on that woman's heart!

If I'd known it'd be like this, I'd have squeezed tight my piddly heart to offer
          you a drink! Would you like one?

(Like someone who keeps offering even though you have nothing to give)

Naked Body

DAY SIXTEEN

"There will be no more night, no need for the lamplight or
sunlight."
—*Book of Revelation 22:5*

Clearness that knows every nook of your body, even the parts you don't
know about, has arrived
Clearness like eyes that have fallen into orgasm has arrived, lifting up the
blanket
Clearness with a dreamlike chemical symbol has arrived, where your soul
with a dreamlike chemical symbol dwells
Clearness of the night that has skipped its dinner has arrived

Something like the clear eagle on your back
Something like the clear toenail inside your dark throat

Like the falling frail twilight and
the rising frail dawn
certain light caves in, certain light soars and embraces

Something like the silvery alligator in your throat
Something like the silvery mosquito on your face

Something like the abrupt opening of the windows of the sea after waking
up from a lifetime of sleep

You'll see the mornings of the world all at once

Your body chemistry will change like the salmon's that has reached the sea

Now that you have died
you need to take your shoes off
Now that you have taken them off, you have no shadow
A voice emerges from the center of a beam of light

You can see the clearness even with your eyes closed, even clearer with your eyes open, you cannot embrace it, you cannot hit it. It clears the blood, washes the face clean, the clearness that lived hidden inside you from the beginning of time, heart to heart. Like hands dipped in honey, semen, the white shadow of the future. The clearness that you cannot see forever has arrived sticky, sticky.

(Abandoned by you
Peeled off from you)

A Grave

A woman is lying on her side, holding on to a round boat

A well that can't be hidden
burst after roaming in the blood
She laughed all day long
clasping her burst vein
The dead woman laughed then cried
for every moment in life was so hilarious

Sunlight was toted down below
in a bucket attached to the umbilical cord

Then a jar full of tears surfaced
Like someone who cleans high-rises
you hung on to the window outside your body
and wiped off your tears

You came from the world over there
but now you're pregnant with that world

Like a newborn on an operating table
the woman who shoved her own neck into the grave
looks at selfies on her phone

even laughing faces of the burial mounds' green hats

Black Fishnet Gloves
DAY EIGHTEEN

In the pitch-black night, a flame shoots up in the middle of the field
The house on fire is like a rose kneaded from crimson water
like a boat lit in the middle of the night sea
like a bier going up in flames in the sky
but inside that blazing flower
a man who wants to die after killing a woman is in flames
In the morning when you awake, the charred house is like a soiled
         bunched-up rag
like a clot of hair stuck on the bloodied hammer when you were struck
like a dirty black hole pulsating beneath the man's eyebrows
like dog hair that dangles down, stuck to the black hole
Filthy ash sticks to your lips

Winter's Smile

DAY NINETEEN

It's cold, for you've come out from a warm body
It's bright, for you've come out from a dark body
It's lonely, for you've lost your shadow

Icy, like soil dug out from a flower pot
Sunny, like the sunlight fish stare at beneath the sheet of ice
Hot, like when lips touch a frozen door knob
Cold again, a bulb-like heart is half frozen

Cold again, as if zero is divided by zero
            a glass divided by glass

It's alright, alright
for you're already dead

The place where you've shed yourself, the cold arrived, drained of all the
        red from your body

I Want to Go to the Island

DAY TWENTY

You leave for the island in the middle of the night.
You get on the ferry, dragging along a small bag.
It's midnight and you're bored. You can't fall asleep.
You go out on the deck. The vast sky and ocean are a black mirror. It
        wavers.
You think about the sleeping fish inside the black mirror.
You think about the gluttony of the vast mirror that leaves nothing behind,
        not even a single shadow.
You ponder, What if starting tomorrow the days without sunrise continue?
Then we'd be inside this black mirror 24 hours a day, and who'd dip a pen
        into the mirrorwater to write about us?
Why is there so much ink for writing?
You head to the cafeteria to shake off your ominous thoughts.
You might have heard the ship floating on black water sobbing sadly.
You receive a phone call after midnight.
The call's about the emptiness of your being gone.
This is the thousandth call.
But emptiness over there is transmitted to you in spite of the calls.
You go into the hallway and pick up the receiver and sing the oldest song
        you know into it.
You set a time for your song to be sent.
So someone feeling empty can hear the song as soon as she opens her eyes
        the next morning.
But you doze off as if you're stepping into the mirrorwater, as you listen to
        the sounds the sleeping bodies make.
For the thousandth time the same seat, same posture, same bodies, same
        smell, same room.
An emptiness walks into the mirrorwater. She's weeping, caressing, and
        calling your name.
The light from the lighthouse dims and you awake from your sleep.
Because you heard the announcement for breakfast.
It's your morning call.
The same menu, same table, same radish kimchi, same taste, same sound,
        same feeling.

You look out the window. Bright sea. Clear sky. You're relieved.
You're almost there.
The sun is high up in the sky and the sea is calm. Wash your face, pack your
        bags, then it's time to disembark.
And darkness.
For the thousandth time you don't reach the island.
You won't be able to reach the island anytime soon.
The moment you think that arrival is near
you board the ferry in the middle of the night, dragging along a small bag.
The sound of the horn from the departing boat makes your heart tremor
Again, it's midnight and you're bored. You can't fall asleep.
You go out on the deck.
The vast sky and ocean are a black mirror.

Smell

Grasshoppers, dragonflies, mosquitoes, and beetles hide
The sky slips away high up
The hills crawl to the bottom
The frogs leap into the grave
The phone rings
You receive the pitch-black darkness before the call
From the receiver the sound of darkness weeping
the sound of wind escaping
the trembling voice of
torrential rain

Night pours out from the showerhead
As you reach out your hand to the sinking night
the rotting birds' dark blood

The unbearable reign of smell, except in death
The unbearable disease of sight, except in death

Someone dead sits at the desk and crinkles paper

A cold winter night for the people of the North Pole
They gnaw on birds that have been buried in the ground wrapped in
        bearskin
the red birds that smell like their own heads

Seoul, Book of the Dead

DAY TWENTY-TWO

Listen, listen to the voice of the mountain of the North
The candlelight inside you is extinguished

Depart!
The moment the first intravenous needle of farewell pricks you
the sky made from your sensations, covering your body, lifts up
The Achilles tendon of the sky breaks

Your body is now fog floating above sleep
Your face is a cloud floating above your body
Your thoughts are the smoke of grilling meat
Your torment is a scream, a breath, escaping from you

Listen, listen carefully to the voices of the snowy mountain peaks
Don't look back. If you do, you will turn into a stone that sinks into a
        nightmare
Don't cry. If you do, you will be reborn as the bedsore of comatose citizens
Listen carefully to the echoes of my words on your distant eardrums
No one will miss you
Fly away freely
When light arrives, offer your eyes
When wind arrives, offer your ears

If you're still there after giving everything away listen to what I say

Your house flutters like a ribbon on long hair
Hurry, depart!

Before somebody else's candle is lit in your body

Lack of Air

As you let go of yourself
you became tinier than a piece of thread
you became so tiny that no one saw you
moreover no one could tell
when you were stuck to somebody's nape

As you let go of yourself
you became as big as the sky
you became so large that you didn't recognize yourself
moreover no one could tell
when you descended as a cloud
when an eyeball was attached to each dew drop

The spectacle of living far from home without a body!
The spectacle of roaming after death as a faint adverb!

Who? Who was it? A suffocating flesh-like cloud came down
and a thread-like temple blew in the wind
You tried to grab the temple
but your hand was so big you couldn't close it

In the eye of the typhoon storming in with rain
the temple's light faintly
flickered

Autopsy

DAY TWENTY-FOUR

Sister's crying, Brother's crying
Why did you leave when it's not your turn yet?

In your room, two bottles of *soju* and a box of sleeping pills
*I can't swallow the pills because my throat hurts**
That's why I can't sleep
Whenever I drink, I hit my mom, hit my sister, hit my brother
Even if I take sleeping pills
it hurts hurts hurts
Revenge revenge revenge
My eyeballs roll back even in my sleep

Under my blanket soldiers in blue outfits march with guns with bayonets
Bloodshot eyeballs roll around in my crotch
The soldiers' yelling lives inside the cast of my broken arm

They beat the shit out of me
They stabbed the shit out of me

Yet they're the ones who are crying. My mom cries, my sister cries, my
        brother cries, my son cries

I wake up from my dream and get out of bed
I hear my mom, sister, brother wailing in the living room

They say I'm dead

* From Cho Yong-bom's "A Psychological Study of Suicide Prevention and
  Societal Support for the Participants of the Democratic Movement, May
  1980 Gwangju Uprising."

Every Day

Where are you going?
You naked angel,
you days of the day,
with wings piddlier than a housefly's

At our house the fly's blue wings
buzz out from the shithole
then buzz back in

Where are you going?
You stinky angel
Ghost, you've lost your wings
The stench of your fingers
The stench of the elderly living alone
In the morning, filthy flowers bloom inside your eyes!
They burrow through your black pupils
Creepy pistils and stamen protrude from them!

At night, inside the ambulance
death death death
I can see the road that you're on
but there's one thing that I don't know
Where are you going?
With wings piddlier than those floating in tepid bathwater
attached to your armpits,
where are you going?

My winter days, my spring days have passed
while I stuff you into my drawer
Really, where are you going
after opening all the drawers of your body?
You tread on bloodied water, one step, two steps,
then finally you lie under the knife?

In this world there are Five Ws & One H for "How," cubes, cuboids,
living rooms, bedrooms, wood coffins, steel coffins, gold coffins

You filthy days
Each hour, the hour of beating
has passed while you repainted in black
the world that was painted in light
So, where are you going
with a red foreclosure notice stuck to your back?
You naked angel
You wicked ghost

You betrayer, I miss you!

The blind bird crashes into the sky and dies!

Mommy of Death

Mommy doesn't know but you do
In the corner of Mommy's heart, a small black mole lifts its head
It becomes a song. A fabulous solo roams desperately looking for death
A song graceful like the deep autumn night

The endless greetings of the dead. The interior is all like that
On top of the flowing song, a bird spits and flies away
Mommy's irises incubate under the ground and the hatched irises float
      about like underground stars
You know everything. For you are Mommy's death

Mommy doesn't know but you do
A crow has built a nest on top of Mommy's hair
Inside Mommy's body that stands like a handless grandfather clock, infants
      doing handstands wait forever ticktockticktock for their next life
The black goats inside Mommy's ears wait to feed on her eardrums
The fluttering wings of two dead birds on Mommy's feet. The rotten smell
You know everything. You who've been banished from Mommy's insides
      know everything
The cold naked black sky is like the ragged feet of a migratory bird yanked
      from a warm body, fleeing to the North Pole
What's the point of flying when the sky is the inside of a grave?
You know everything. For you are the Mommy of death

aeiou

Grandmother does dishes and crazy you eat your breakfast
You stop eating and you're still crazy, so you throw a bowl of sugar onto the
      wooden floor
White sugar spills out like sticky stardust
At that moment, the strange sound of a tiny hiccup comes from the kitchen
As soon as you hear it crazy you know that Grandmother is dead
Strangely you knew
At that moment you also knew that the "craziness" fell off of you
You watch the "craziness" lump up and roll away like the black droppings
      of a fawn
You lay Grandmother on top of the spilt sugar
You dial 911 then hang up and stare at your toe prints on the floor
Four, five round toe prints on a mound of snow-like sugar

The fawn circling its grandmother shot dead
on top of the snow is surrounded by hoof prints
pronounced as the foreign letters a e i o u

Already

You are already born inside death
(echoes 49 times)

Dinner Menu

There's no rice in Mommy's rice jar
There's no money in Mommy's purse
There's no fire in Mommy's kitchen

Today, Mommy cooks pan-fried hair
Yesterday, Mommy cooked braised thighs
Tomorrow, Mommy will cook sweet and sour fingers

In the kitchen, a knife bangs against the cutting board
In the kitchen, a bone steeps in broth
In the kitchen, thighs are deep fried

There's Mommy inside Mommy's rice jar
There's Mommy inside Mommy's purse
There's Mommy inside Mommy's kitchen
There's Mommy beneath Mommy's knife

Your mommy is that riverbank of your childhood
Your mommy is that trail of your childhood

When you go along the trail all alone past the riverbank

Mommy's weak voice: My daughter,
you've come, hurry, come in
When the door opens,
an empty stove, cold air

In your mommy's kitchen
your deflated hungry stomach
is hanging on the black wall
like a rusted frying pan

Tonight, you'll fry Mommy's
hands in that frying pan

A Gift
DAY THIRTY

The only thing you can give birth to yourself is, your death
Nurture it, give birth to it as a tasty plump death

The only thing you can give back to yourself is, your death
It's like Mommy's milk you've suckled on your whole life, the thing you
       need to give back after you wean yourself from it

The only thing you can offer yourself is, your death
Preserve it from decay then serve it when it's absolutely fresh

The only thing you can undress for yourself is, your death
Finally your first black wings flap when your body is ripped apart

The most difficult thing for you to part from is your death
In the end, the thing that you must return to yourself is, your death

Hiccups

Stepdaughter silence that used to live inside you begins to sing softly

She sings like a stutterer who doesn't stutter when singing
as if unexpectedly only the consonants have been extracted from the song
like the way a hiccup continues after a hiccup
She wants to go down the stairs
deep inside your body where the fainted fainting lives

Click, click, the door latch

Stepmom has died. Just now
Stepdaughter lies under the ground and sings. She sings quietly

Stepdaughter silence that you've locked up
underground your whole life pulls you
When the silence you've hidden deep inside your crotch
stops breathing, the world that finally becomes visible
drags you across the floor, asks you to come down below
like an underground stream
It convulses, burrowing into you

Stepmom is dead
Stepmom who sent me to her previous husband is dead
Stepmom who sent me to her previous lover is dead

A low note no one has ever sung before

Open your hands under the light
Pebble-like eyes stare at you
The two pebbles are heavier than this world
Currents overlap the black pebbles that will sink you down

Next, it's your turn, your turn to sing
(I raised you so lovingly)

(I hid you so carefully)

Stepmom has died. Just now
The clear silence of the shimmering crazy bitch
lifts up the house
Throws down the house
The underground stream gushes out

When the hiccups subside the horizon pulls up its zipper

A Lie

Press the button, and it's winter. No one can set up house in winter. It's unbelievably quiet. It's unbelievably clean. From the sky above, the shattered window glass glitters like gems. Imagine all the idle buses without tires at the station. The stars die, the moon dies. White chickens faint on top of the snow. Chicken coops collapse. Imagine a city where no one wakes up even when morning arrives. All you have to do is press the button. It's easier than poking embroidery with a needle. Not a moment to let out a scream. You can throw away yesterday's bus ticket. You don't have to carry the old sack on your back, no more farewells. Bid farewell to farewells. Only the white ash soars. Just press the button, and there's a fallen tree on top of a fallen person, the fallen wind on top of the fallen tears, the fallen water overflows on top of the fallen building. Press the button, and your filthy secrets are buried forever like the breath of the dead. It's totally fair. Don't laugh when you get there. The loneliness of a loner now vanishes. That's why the lonely ending presses the button. The loneliest ending in the world. How incredibly fortunate. So hurry, press the button, said Mister.

Death is the only lie in the world!

Crows' feathers are pink! Even the river is pink!

By the River of Formalin
DAY THIRTY-THREE

Brain inside the test tube is still alive
Looks like it's writing poetry
It's plunging into a blurry image
It's opening the gate to grandparents' house like a wind
The instant it runs into the embrace of dead grandmother

Its missing eyes open
Its missing body hallucinates a black stick whacking its head

Brain inside the test tube is hurting

You're outside of you
Your outside hurts

Missing toes hurt
Scattered rooms hurt. Your heart hurts

Brain inside the test tube scratches its body all over with its ten fingers
Scratches till the skin breaks

Brain inside the test tube takes off
It rides the subway, rides the bus, takes a cab
and exits the test tube
It departs swaying
like a head inside the plastic bag of a serial killer

I want to tell you, tell you everything
but my mouth stays shut
my hands shake
where did my shoes go?

Roots of the dark-blue night descend into the test tube
Everyone has left the lab
Brain inside the test tube mutters

Whitest monster inside me
has a blue nightdress on

You're transparent like water
and soft
but you're fatal like the blue saliva of a poisonous snake

Brain inside the test tube is a bystander's brain, a survivor's brain

Brain inside the test tube always wants to bang its head against the wall and
        weep
Brain submerged in formalin river sways back and forth

An obscure place like this poem
An ambiguous place like this poem
A disinfected place like this poem

Brain inside the test tube puts on its formalin hat and thinks intently

Why does my outside always hurt?

Why do my missing feet hurt?
Why does the riverbed that props up my feet crumble?

Someone who has set himself on fire stands at the rail of a bridge

Brain inside the test tube is screaming
Brain inside the test tube has gone mad

What am I to do?

What can I do to forget all this?

Death Swarmswarms

Above you
Below you
Next to you
Beneath you
Beside you
Beyond you
Behind you
Inside you

Should I say someone is scratching the night with a razor blade?
Say each scratch becomes bright momentarily?

Say you are weeping?
Say you are breast-feeding the whimpering young deaths?

Say you can't sleep at all?
Say we've just met?

Say you are banging your head against the wall?
Say your screams fill up like crystals?
Say the hard, clear crystals have already risen all the way up to your throat?

Lowering the Coffin
DAY THIRTY-FIVE

The wind that gently ties thin streaks of rain into moist ribbons and pins
     them to your nipples has arrived

Ticklish yellow piss, yellow cloud that drizzles down the gutter has arrived

The girl pulled out from you cries under the eaves

Dead from childhood, your older sister pinches your belly with her frail
     fingernails

Ghost, you break off green fingernails, Spring, you're a step ahead of me

Playwithme playwithme, twirling skinny pinkies

Spiky sprouts burrow through your teary eyes

The smell of your sister's barely-showing underwear, floating about in the
     air

Then the smell of her rotten grave panties when they land on your nose

Broth made from ribs rises and falls in your body. The ribs are your coffin,
     carrying you around

Someone is lowering your coffin into a deep hole—hazylazy skylark—
     someone is lowering your coffin

Dark flesh-colored tree gulps down a sip of wine in the midst of lifting up
     your sister's skirt

Why haven't you left? Every morning the sky, the blue vein slaps you hard

Before your skinny fingers are born, the cherry-blossom-wind bursts your
     pink cheeks in their white mourning dresses

The tire marks of a Cadillac hearse zigzag across the green barley field

The mountain stretches and yawns, lifting the hydrangea blossoms from its
    belly

Flowers chirp like birds with blood-stained beaks, they keep spitting their
    bloodied teeth

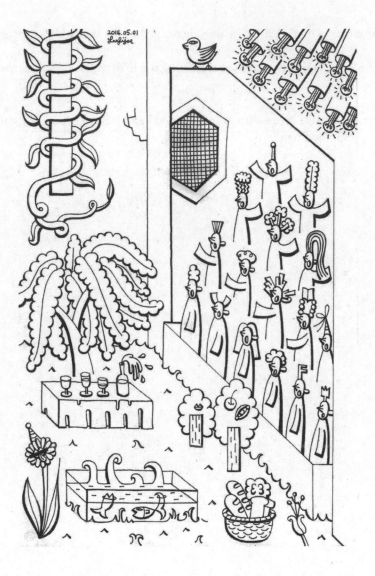

Lord No

That you live with Lord No
he who descends from the mountain
That you sleep with the one who created you
You eat at the same table with
the one who claims to feed and raise you
the one who strips bare the world he has made
You live with him who
slaps your mommy's back
crinkles your mommy's brain map and
secretly locks the door to the outside world and discards the key
That you fall asleep with Lord No
who shouts, Earn your keep!

You keep shouting in your head
I was born alone!
I have nothing to do with you!
Your sibling couldn't eat anything in front of him
She could only weep, vomit, and think of the waves of music
She wrapped herself in them
ran around in bed like a hedgehog
huffing and puffing from aphasia

Lord No does not Lord No and none and not at Lord No thus Lord No does
       not
Not none never Lord No nevertheless
Lord No who is not Lord No is never Lord No thus Lord No is Lord No of
       Lord No
Not Lord No is not Lord No thus Lord No is Lord No who will none to Lord
       No
Not Lord No is not Lord No thus Lord No is Lord No who will never Lord
       No to Lord No
Lord No who is not Lord No Lord No to Lord No is not Lord No thus is not
       Lord No

Lord No whom Lord No never not is not Lord No thus never none not to
      Lord No
Lord No who is not Lord No is never Lord No thus Lord No is Lord No who
      will not to Lord No
Lord No who does not none is not Lord No thus Lord No is Lord No of Lord
      No hence is Lord No who will not Lord No
Lord No who has never Lord No and none Lord No is not Lord No thus
      Lord No is Lord No of Lord No
None to Lord No then no to Lord No and never thus not Lord No by Lord
      No is not not Lord No is not Lord No to Lord No
Do not and not, Lord No is Lord No of Lord No from Lord No, Lord No who
      did not to Lord No was none like Lord No

That you live with Lord No
that you must end the prayer in his son's name
that you must live with the one who made the law
yet with his crocodile-like eyes
he tells you to beware of a snake-like friend
That you live forever with Lord No who slaps your face
that you live with the naked light
who asks you whenever you undress
aren't you ashamed?

A Lullaby

The mother of the child coddled her dead child in her arms

She sang a lullaby

This is the contents of her lullaby:

Sleep, sleep my baby, die soon so you'll be at ease, so you won't have to cry

The mother of the child dug a hole in the middle of her room and buried
     her child

She also buried her child in the ceiling. Buried her in the wall. Buried her in
     her pupils

Nobody knew the name of the child's mother, but they knew the child's
     name

A Crow Flew Over the Cuckoo's Nest

Yourfatherinheaven. Belovedbullshitfather. Heasksforthechild. Atnightthe snow hiddendeepinheaven fallsflakebyflakesecretly likethewayamummy takesoffitsownbandages we'reallanakedchild whenthebandagescomeoff DoIpaint thecolumnsofthehousewiththechild'sblood? Thehouseiscrying. Thehouseistrembling. Yourfatherinheaven. Belovedbullshitfather. This child. Thischild. (I write. I write like an abductor. This child this child.)

Icicle Glasses

DAY THIRTY-NINE

The thing that death gave you—
your face leaks
your face overflows

Your face is the grave of your nose
your face is the grave of your ears
your face is the grave of your face
once again your face overflows uncontrollably

The subzero temperature grows on your face then dies
(You were underground from the moment you were born)

The air that sticks to your eyes is as cold as the knife blade
the wind that sticks to your heart is as hot as the palm of a hand

You want to shout that you miss me
but there is another ground beneath the ground

You wish to sing solo but you are stuck in the chorus
In this world there is no ear that can make out your voice

Love sickness, the chronic illness of the ghosts!
Love sickness appears daily like the first dawn!

You hang your eyeballs to the ground and plead
You beg to be let in
To have your face overlap with my face
That my tongue is your tongue
That you shed my tears

Water streams out
You hallucinate
You go mad

Such Painful Hallucination
DAY FORTY

Listen, listen carefully to what I have to say
Now you'll see the world inside your glasses

You'll know what the water is saying inside you
You'll know what the fire is saying inside you

You'll see the three eyes dangling from you
You'll see your rage as the other
You'll see the four eyes dangling from you
You'll see your anxiety as the other
You'll see the eight heads dangling from you
You'll see your fear as the other
You'll see the dogs inside you
You'll see the pigs inside you

You'll see the you who became a triangle
You'll see the you who became a rectangle

You'll pass a tribe of endless patterns made from your voices that never
      evaporate

Listen, listen without fear
for it's the night of you raging like the influenza
for it's the night of the mourning outfit giving birth to you at the bottom of
      the well
for it's the night of you blooming for the hundredth, a hundred and one
      times
for it's the night of death panting repeatrepeatrepeatedly from hunger
for it's the night of all the holes of your body packing up to move

for it's the night of you who have died inside you awakening
for it's the night of the snails, the wingless bats
waking up faceless, brainless, their bodies slippery at the bottom of the well

for it's the night of the dead you of yesterday and the dead you of the day
      before jumping rope
each time you jump up a dead giraffe, a dead dragon, a dead hen falls to the
      bottom

Look, look carefully without fear

Marine Blue Feathers
DAY FORTY-ONE

"Twenty-eight yogis will come out from your brain and greet you.
They'll be carrying various tools, and their heads will be the heads
of various animals."

—*Tibetan Book of the Dead*

1
This world is my death, so I lie down with my left and right wrists on top of
     one another
I float with the back of my head facing the sky

My spine becomes as skinny as a pen
I cover my thin, prostrated pen-like body with a blanket

You watch your shadow plunge down in the shape of a hen toward the
     surface of the paper
Why is your soul human when your spine is a pen and your shadow is a
     hen?
Is it true that poets see a piece of filthy paper at the time of their death?

2
A blue hen big enough to reach the sky cackles
but when I came home there was a crinkled blue paper under my pillow

A tiger roared and attacked as if it could swallow the entire continent
but a motherless moth with striped wings was crying outside my room

I flew beyond the sound barrier and struck the sky like a tornado
but a beetle was circling in front of my door

3
but your grave's ceiling is a mercury mirror
but your grave is so shallow that you can't stand or even sit up in it
but you can see your breath in there
but your lovely breasts are pressed down by the ceiling

4
The ghost inside your skull is spilling water like a kettle
Your temporal lobe become active and your eyelashes flicker like the
          eyelashes of the blue hen

A voice scorches your hair like electricity
A voice beats your thoughts like a club

That strange voice is not human
That thing perches on your ears and cackles
That thing flies around inside your skin
That thing is neither solid, liquid, nor gas
That thing is barbaric, you can't open or close it

(Are you saying that you're still a fetus, growing your liver with the sounds
          inside your mommy?)

5
The flying blue hen lays an egg inside its body
The blue hen clucks, I can't endure I can't endure

The crown of the blue hen is tall and its beak is long so its head gets buried
          in its chest
The blue hen clucks, I can't endure I can't endure

It looks as if the blue hen is enduring the time it takes for fish from the sea
          to evolve

The feet disappear in the last phase of its evolution
You don't have to walk at all
You don't have to sleep or eat

The blue hen clucks inside a huge hole in the back of your head
The blue sky opens under your left eyelid

But the blue hen's tiny feet are buried inside each page
Whenever you turn the page its huge wings flutter!

So is this place the footless corpse of the blue sky?
So is this place the blue, eternal stillness of your breath?

The hen is as blue and vast as the blue sky!
I can't endure. I can't endure!

Name

Your dead lover wants to meet you. Wants to meet you at a café. Wants to meet you in a restroom. Wants to meet you at a hospital. Wants to meet you overseas. If not here or there, wants to meet you in bed. Just for a brief moment. There's no use avoiding it. Tells you to come outside the window, for a brief moment. Just wants to see your face.

Your dead lover asks why you've come. That it's not time for you to meet yet. But since you've come she asks you to lie down. Asks you to sleep since you're lying down. Asks you to leave since you've slept. Tells you to put on your shoes properly. Tells you that you don't need to shout so much. That you don't need to fall down so much. No need for your knees to get scraped at all.

Your dead lover comes to you. Even though she doesn't open the door. Even though she's not carrying a bag. Even though she's not wearing shoes. Even though she's not coughing. She wouldn't be able to come to you so often if she were alive. She still shows up without an appointment. Even though she's undressed. Even though she's buried in the ground.

You walk beneath the sea that's filled with your lover. Beneath the raging sea filled with your lover. You walk beneath the sea, unable to breathe, unable to stop breathing. You walk beneath the stormy sea. Beneath the raining sea. You walk gasping through the vast oscillating blue, the sea ceiling, the sea floor, the sea wall, the sea window. You walk beneath the sea and see your lover whichever direction you turn your head. No one can see from the outside, but several meters beneath the sea two whales are having a bloody fight.

Your dead lover wants to drink tea with you. Wants to eat with you. Wants to wash her face with you. Wants to play with you. Wants to travel with you in your dreams. Becomes more and more callous. You were trying to find a way to break up with your lover, but your lover removes her hands from her eyes and asks you what your name is. She asks, Haven't we met before?

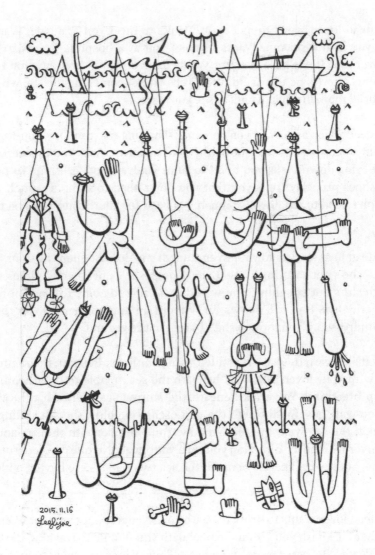

2015. 11. 16
Leeljoe

A Face

World without a sound. Untouchable, flat world. When death dawns, world turns into a hard mirror. Faraway world of hope. The mirror reflects all things like the face of someone whose insides are dead. The shape of a woman appears in the mirror. Now you've become toeless feet. Now you've become fingerless hands. You've become a noseless, mouthless face. Your insides that are so far away yet close, the forest in your hair, light enters the rocky moon, and the sea wavers in your shoes. Birds fly up your sleeves and a horse weeps in your pants. The dissolving outline of a woman, a woman trapped inside a round mirror, a woman whose tongue is melting inside her mouth cries inside the slippery edge of the freezing mirror. The full moon wanes. Whenever the sleek mirror flashes in her eyes, something heavy and transparent stomps on her face. The hard world can be seen but not entered. The world is white like a movie screen but with clenched fists. Perhaps the woman's faint arms are still stirring it.

A Doll

A doll watches another doll set on fire
watches it burn across the river then moves in closer
sees the scalp of the doll burning

Someone takes another someone away
Who put your doll on top of the woodpile?
Your body's all burnt up but you don't return
like a guest who asks to spend the night
then never wakes up

Who scooped up and drank your mother's breast milk?
Who stole you and placed your doll in the stroller?
Who raised your clueless bones and sent them to school?

When you look at the photo of the outdoor cremation site in Varanasi,
          there's
perhaps a doll, perhaps a human, perhaps you, perhaps me, perhaps tears,
perhaps sweat, under a yellow blanket, a crushed thing stuck to the
          stretcher

Underworld

The dead without faces

run out like patients

when the door of the intensive care unit opens

carrying pouches of heart, pouches of urine

The dead running toward the path to the underworld

turn into stone pillars when they look back and their eyes meet their past

The dead in their sacks look out with eyes brimming with salt water

The dead become pillars of water as their tears melt their bones
The dead, gone forever, departed before you,
pull amniotic sacs over their heads and get in line to be born again
and say that they need to learn their mother tongue all over again
You're not there when they awake or even when they eat breakfast
When the dead swarm down the mountain
like children who pour out of the door of the first-grade room
carrying their notebooks and shoe bags

a four-ton bronze bell with a thousand names of the dead engraved on it
        dangles from the helicopter
The helicopter flies over a tall mountain to hang the bell at a temple hidden
        deep in the mountains

Asphyxiation

DAY FORTY-SIX

Hence breath
Then breath
Next breath
Subsequent breath
Because breath
Such breath
And breath
Same breath
Thereafter breath
Thus breath
Always breath
Eventually breath
Perpetually breath
Yet breath
However breath
Therefore breath
In spite of breath
Breath till the bitter end

Death breathes and you dream but

it's time to remove the ventilator from death
it's time to shatter the dream with a hammer

Heart's Exile

DAY FORTY-SEVEN

Who's drawing up the water inside your body?

Who's having sex inside your body?

Outside the window a man's and a woman's shoes
plop plop plop plop down

(Did you know that
our existence is lumped together by the sound of our weeping?)

Who's playing the pipe organ inside you?

Who's shivering in the mud inside you?

Who's heaving up water beneath the rock layers inside you?

(The woman silently walking on the roof of a certain century
cradles her pregnant belly
and rests for a moment on the terrace

The lenses made of tears caress the window)

Moon Mask

DAY FORTY-EIGHT

Now you have completely taken off your face

The full white moon rises in the east

A thousand masks float on the thousand rivers of the north, south, east,
    west

Don't

The warm buoyant breaths don't miss you
The winds that have left for reincarnation before you, that brush against
        the lips of your childhood don't miss you

The winter, the woman's ice-heart, dead from sickness, drifting away in the
        infinite blue sky
with thin needles stuck all over it doesn't miss you

The leaves blow away, leaving their prints on the frozen river and

the one-hundred, two-hundred-story high buildings crumble all at once
        and

the spectacles with spectacles, shoes with shoes, lips with lips, eyebrows
        with eyebrows, footprints with footprints swept into a huge drawer
        don't miss you

The river is frozen eighty centimeters deep, a tank passes over it, and the
        fish beneath the ice don't miss you

The dog tied to the electric pole in front of the tobacco shop for fourteen
        years doesn't miss you

While the big wind takes away thousands of women dead from madness

the sound of the "you's" of your whole life, your hair falling

all of the winter landscape, wailing and wielding its whip doesn't miss you

Thousands, hundreds of thousands, millions of snow flurries don't miss you

Don't descend all over the world, howling, murmuring, searching for your
        snowman-like body buried in the snow, don't miss you and say love
        you or whatever as if unfolding a beautifully folded letter

Don't miss you just because you're not you and I'm the one who's really you

Don't miss you as you write and write for forty-nine days with an inkless
       pen

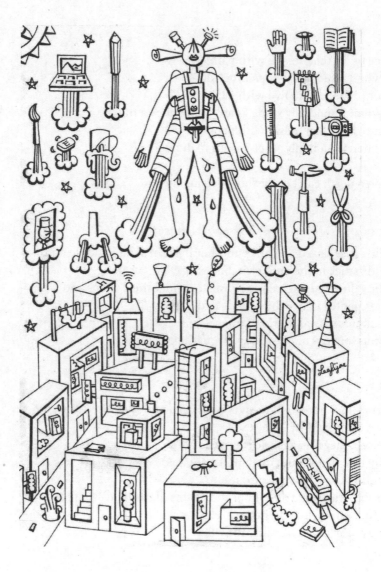

Face of Rhythm

§

Better to die than to live with pain
but when it suddenly stops I feel alone
Better to die than to live with pain
but when it suddenly stops I can't remember a thing
Better to die than to live with pain
but when it suddenly stops I want to die

for even death can't enter this deep inside me

§

Eyelids that closed one after another lived in a mud puddle and
Eyelids stuck to the mud twitched and
Eyelids fluttered like moths trying to unfold their wings and
Bodies panted under the eyelids and
Rainclouds moved in from faraway and
Lisping sounds could be heard from the puddle and

§

Dearest, look at the white stars pouring down from the afternoon sky
Listen to the SOS of each star
Up close, they are gigantic rocks
So big that they let out deafening screams
plunging toward me, toward me
Dearest, a thousand, ten thousand beams of sunlight sting me
The hidden world of twinkling white stars
Dearest, can't you hear it? My SOS?

§

I've split into two but I'm alive
I've split into five but I'm alive
I've become powder but I'm alive

In sync with rhythm, I'm me then not me

A heap of powder puffs puffs, breathing
The edge of its mouth bursts and white powder spews out

It's time for the mother of pain to knead me

§

Woman's body is tied up to rhythm
Woman drags along her barking shadow *kung kung*

Woman says death speaks a foreign language daily
like princes who come to propose from overseas

Woman grins,
Do princes really need I love you to be translated?

§

Citizens laughed inside princess's head
It was useless giving orders to arrest those who laughed
for the laughter belonged to the dead
It was recorded long ago
like a laugh track

An order was given to make princess laugh
but no one showed up

§

Peachsink
Peachslippers
Likeanadolescentgirlthesinkgrowssoft hair
Peachsoap
Peachtoothpaste
Smell of sickly breath nearby
Smell of peach
Smell of bent knees
Peach needle
at Eden's peachorchard before going under general anesthesia

Smell of cheap peaches as I go down the basement levels –1 –2 –3 –4

A young nursing assistant with a shaving knife comes over to shave peach
      hair

§

Prince is in agony and princess is in pain
Prince is in mourning and princess is in pain
Prince is in consciousness and princess is in nerve
Prince lectures and princess screams
Prince's agony is princess, princess's pain is nameless
Prince does melody, princess does rhythm
Prince does lyrics, princess does beats

Father! It wasn't me. He's the one who chose me.
Father! When I eat, pain eats too

Princess Nakrang clutches my face inside her pocket

§

The hitting side is silent mob
The beat-up side is howling mob
The hitting side is water cannon, billy club, riot shield
The beat-up side is a mere scream
The hitting side is Hammurabi-like justice
Attack anything that moves!
Attack even if nothing moves, of course!

Why on earth are they fighting inside me?

Sky is trembling
Streets scream it hurts hurts
Flag flares up from my face

Who's hurting the most?

The square gets beat up and shakes shakes

§

When mommy is sick, all of my childhood gets sick

When I'm sick, all the days I've never visited get sick

I've never learned pain's planetary language but
planetary leaves keep talking to me
planetary newborns keep talking to me

Holy Mother of pain! Unrelenting Holy Mother! Beloved Holy Mother's
        teeth!

§

Whale floats about in the night sea
Whale cries alone, laughs alone, drifts far
inside to a darker place

§

Whale floats about inside my black pupil
Whale drags me
to the inside far away from myself

§

I get prescriptions for this and that
If these meds work then it's this illness and if those meds work then it's
        that illness
Doctors' names are used for naming illnesses
But patients' names have never once been used
Illness that lived and died with a patient is nameless

Massage therapist says: It's not an illness but a knotted line. It needs to be
        straightened
Mommy says: It's not an illness but your aunty
But, Mommy, you are an only child

§

Mommy, droplets of water are falling from the IV
Millions of faces are swarming inside a single droplet
Faces enter my face
Faces wail
Faces in soiled diapers cry mommymommy

Faces want to be born
Faces are in pain though nameless

§

There's a gravel pavement
I'm driving on it
Do Not Enter. I pass the sign, swerving
A deceased poet
As soon as I meet her I know I'm in a foreign country

There's a slippery freeway
I'm driving on it
Dead End. I see the sign but speed away
A deceased poet
As soon as I see her I know I'm inside the poet

§

Get in when the skipping rope touches the ground! I hear a sound. Rope is
sick. Sickness blooms. Soon the rope takes off into the air. Now's the time to
make it out of here. But again, Get in! The rope whips the ground and the
pain soars. Aches again. It's worse than death. Worse than nothing. But the
rope ascends again. Just then the sky expands and Buddha's shrine shoots
up. But again, Get in! I get beat up. Let go of your hands! I shout, not knowing
that my hands are tied with rope. But I yell again, Get in! Pain swarms in.
Circus dwarf is playing with a whip.

§

I carry a sick doll and make her stand in front of the sunset
I'lltakeitout takeitout
If the body's sickness dies

doll also dies
Sun goes down, weeping

I carry a sick doll and make her stand on water
makemesleep makemesleep
I could go on living
just seeing your face once a day
But for now
makemesleep makemesleep
makemesleep more deeply than the reflection of the forest's
temple lamp on the lake
makemesleep so deep that pain won't wake up

Somehow a crow enters my body and can't find its way out
it hops up hops up hops up
Upper chin and lower chin are shut; sound of beatings every time they open
Crimson lake begins begins begins
pucker pucker its lips

If dolly dies I'll cover her with a white sheet
Dolly begins to wail as if electrocuted

§

Dog that doesn't know it's a dog builds a house inside my head. When it barks, I ache and when I ache, I feel ashamed. I lie to my spoon, lie to my rice bowl, lie to my hair, that the dog is asleep. I weep, hush-a-bye baby. I prostrate and beg. I lie on my back and throw a temper tantrum. I kiss up. Dog, you are ill. Dog passes out when injected with anesthesia. Then slowly wakes up for various reasons: the wind, its tilted head, worries about bad sentences, hyper-alertness. I now focus only on one dog. I can't even turn my head in sleep, for I'm afraid of waking up the dog. Dog is a habitual wife-beater. There's no explanation for it. Explanation is a lie. I carry the dog in the right side of my head and go to the hospital. I say, Dog is barking inside my head. I end my pilgrimage to the hospital. Dwarf's house becomes full when Dog enters it.

§

Someone who has just one head but two bodies came over

Can I stay the night?

A flowering tree with just one flower with two stems came over

Can I bloom overnight then leave?

I scream as they pull at me from both sides

My bulb-root soars up in the air, splitting

§

Every time an egg breaks, a deformed crow flies out
So wretched that there's no word for it
One crow even has a beak attached to its anus

A rabbit brings its litter in search of food
It grabs one with its mouth and drags over another
So wretched that there's no word for it
One bunny even has three ears

Six headless women are hanging from the window
and I'm trying to take off my own body

§

When that day arrives
gall bladders and lymph nodes, hearts and stomachs become mint-
        refreshed
delicate secrets dangle from the dark tree of the flesh farm, giving off an
        intense minty scent

When that day arrives
as if the light in my mouth got thrown onto the tea fields
as if swooning from the green dizziness
gall bladders and lymph nodes, hearts and stomachs asleep inside a bronze
        statue for a thousand years suddenly
spin spin spin

I take a plane to a faraway place and roam all day, then return the next
        morning on an early flight and embrace that most precious day
I buy cigarettes, stick a bottle of booze in my sack and roam the distant
        alleys till dawn then tightly wrap that day as I head out for my
        return flight

That day
that I've wrapped in cloth rumbles like a plane

When that day enters a room for two
when that day becomes bright
as if gall bladders and lymph glands, hearts and stomachs are hanging from
        an alley
butcher shop of some foreign country

as if two clean hospital beds are taking off
tied to the haze rising in front of the plane

When that day arrives
When that day arrives, fleeing from the coop of pain
When that day arrives, tying up your distance and mine

§

A ball made of knotted sounds
bumps against this and that wall
Ball giggles, teeters, bounces
The playground is quiet even though
a dark rat's chasing the ball like a shadow
The new road stops and
peers into the playground

Did I just say wall?
Wall answers, uh-huh uh-huh
Walls are stuck to the whole world

There's something still alive inside the garbage bag left outside behind the
        restaurant

§

I'm in pain, yet I'm told not to worry, that I won't be dying soon

There's only one option
I can't kill the pain
so I must kill myself

I receive news that all living things that have built houses above ground or
        under water
are dead, that the only surviving thing is the thing inside my head
and that's because the news was sent by that thing living inside my head

As my head vibrates boom boom like a drum
a huge dog inside my head suddenly opens its eyes

§

An underwater camera goes off inside the dark water
but it's unable to take any shots
for its flashlight beam only reaches one centimeter

Elevator drops endlessly
drops for several days, drops for several months
drops till it goes from the North Pole to the South Pole

Morning is locked inside a mirror
I'm locked inside night
A relentless standoff all day long
Dog barks in a thousand-year-old castle
A bolt of lightning

§

I enter the confession booth
I need to call out the priest's name, so he'll listen to my final confession
I can't remember his name
I don't know the dark priest's name
Pedro, Andre, Jacob, Matthew, Thomas, James, John, Philip, Bartholomew,
        Thaddeus
Simone, Kerioth, Judah
I call out the name of the twelfth disciple
Next, I call out the Pope's name
John Paul Francis the first, the second, the third, the fourth
the thousandth, the ten-thousandth but it's not the dark priest's name

I'm inside a pitch-black tunnel
A woman recedes like a fairy tale
She's going to hell

I need to call out the priest's name
Only then I'll be able to confess
and find my sins

§

Scream rain pours down
My room spins like a washing machine
I go back and forth from yesterday to my room for the hundredth time
I hear ringring in my ears, electric shock again
I'm conscious but my body feels like wet clothes
Doctors hate such expressions, even readers
Something's tapping on my window
The vibrations from the lightbulb on the wall intensify
I glance, glance back
Someone's waiting for me to break, break then die
I know who that is
Inside the washing machine I imitate the voices of many people
In between my chest afloat in the air and
my other chest stretched out on the bed writhing in pain
a thin silvery line pulsates as if it's about to snap, snap

§

The moment rhythm lifts the princess up in the air
melody dies
Endless lightning bolts of rhythmic beats
With each flash, flash of lightning, swish, swish archangel's wings manifest
As long as the nuclear reactor keeps going
Princess's feet won't drop

§

That feeling of my soul getting yanked
I wonder where my soul hides when I'm sick
My heart feels as if it's getting beat up
Is it because the restless ocean is clumping up?
My heart beats regardless of the pain
It beats spewing out red thread like a red spider
A sinkful of red thread gets submerged in water
My heart beats like a girl marathon runner who only had ramen to eat

Maybe the soul of the bald girl in a hospital gown hanging by the
          windowsill has come to greet me
When the rose in a vase bleeds on my pupils
a song from the radio wraps a bandage over my eyes

I wonder whether the souls of all the people on earth are connected as one

§

New moon rises and a forklift enters the plains inside my head
I feed the blind forklift driver screams one spoonful at a time

The spoon digs under my tongue
to scrape me out, crouched and dark inside the oyster shells

My intestines come up through my dark throat like a snake

§

Those scattering flowers
can't be made from pain

Those scattering birds
can't be flown by pain

Those scattering, scattering sands
the sand above sand above sand
can be made from pain

§

Am I living off on rhythm?
Is rhythm living off on me?
Rhythm isn't a method of existence but a method of lack

I hate this beat that strips my mind
I hate this music that peels my soul

I hate this wave made of mirrors
I keep my eyes shut to avoid seeing dogs in the mirrors

§

I get on the train with a dog in my arms, the dog that used to live on the
        moon
The passengers are as silent as ghosts as if they're inside a webtoon
The train is incredibly bright like a spacecraft blasting off
I stroke the dog's white fur
How were you able to leave the moon?
Soon all the hair on my body stands up and
I'm standing on four feet, licking a woman

§

A breathing drum
Drum wears a coat and trembles

Drum carries shoes and trembles

—fast as much as possible
—as if overly excited
—as if fading, falling

Furthermore, every second a day comes to an end

—speed up again
—*pianissimo subito*
—in the middle breathing gets faster

I look as if I've fallen into a suspense of love
as if every second the plane that's carrying me takes off in your direction

Dog's breath begins from a tiny pain
Breath as big as a house heaves, oscillating
The whole world puts on a thick coat and shoes and trembles
Father, please let me go

A soul as big as the universe wants to leave my body

§

Forsake me when you turn on the ignition for takeoff
Forsake me when the propellers mince the sky
Forsake me when the propellers reach deep inside my skull
Forsake me when the river given to the devil ripples against my lips
Forsake me when the mountain peaks soar like fangs growing out of my
        eyelids

Pain of filthy grass in the descent of winter to come
Pain of bones breaking one by one whenever the eagle's pungent wings are
        spread

Pain of owl that can only open its eyes in the dark
Pain as vertical and deadly as Mount Everest
Forsake me when the pain of Earth that rotates its body once a day swarms
        into the cockpit
Forsake me when the mountains prostrate beneath the night plane
with pouches of pain dangling from them
Forsake me somewhere far far

Dwarf weeps at the feet of pain

Weeps, finally

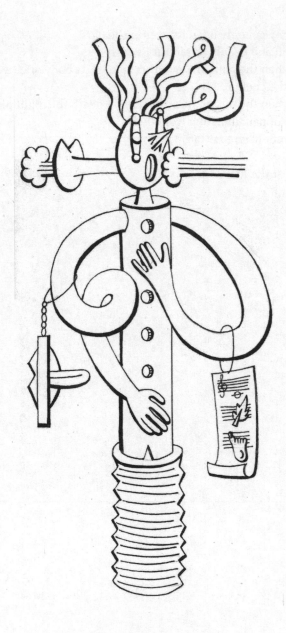

An Interview

Don Mee Choi: *How did you come to write the poems in* Autobiography of Death?

Kim Hyesoon: In April of 2014, a ferry carrying passengers and high school students going on a field trip to an island capsized. All of us, the whole country, couldn't take our eyes off the scene on TV of the slowly sinking ferry. The children had their life jackets on, so if they had been told to leave the boat, they could have survived, but instead the crew instructed them to stay in their cabins and then escaped themselves. The police that came to the rescue were helpless, and the government didn't do a thing and never investigated the tragedy. I teach at a college near the children's school. For a whole year I didn't wear any clothes with bright colors. Going to work every day was like going to a funeral. Besides this ferry incident, there have been many other incidents in our country where people have lost their lives under the violent force of government. While resisting injustice, many have died on a massive scale; and many also have died because they had been unjustly accused. So whenever such unbearable events occurred, I wrote these poems. I also wrote them whenever death was near me or welled up within me. Why does our country make us ashamed for being alive, for surviving those tragic events? I initially titled this collection of poems *Seoul, Book of the Dead*. Then I changed it to *The Sea of Heart*. I kept changing the title nearly every day. Then it occurred to me that all the poems in this collection were written by death, as a kind of autobiography. I came to think that I, we are all part of the structure of death, that we remain living in it. I realized that I'd been kept alive by death. In other words, my existence, my identity didn't begin with birth but with death. I thought to myself that I needed to sing death, perform a rite for death, write death, then bid farewell to it. The way to send death away was to sing with my own death all the death in the sky and on the ground. I wanted nothing to remain for the reader after reading the poems, like nothing remains after mindlessly reciting a multiplication table, like seven times seven is forty-nine. I wanted the poems to vaporize. In other words, I wanted a ghost of collectivity to emerge from the poems.

DMC: *Now that I have arrived in Seoul, my first home, I feel as if I'm invisible. All I do is walk around, looking at wings on various totem animals on old palaces. Even the traditional tiled roofs look like wings to me and also the mountain peaks behind the Gwanghwamun Square. I feel as if I'm floating about in downtown Seoul, looking for a part of myself I had left behind long ago. And since I've been here, I've thought about the Wim Wenders film* Wings of Desire *a lot while translating the poems in* Autobiography of Death. *Perhaps your writing method involved listening to death. I think of ears as wings. Was it like that for you?*

KH: While I was listening to your question, I thought of something amusing. The Korean word for "hearing" is a homonym for the word "possessed," as in possessed by a ghost or spirit; a homonym for "visiting" or "dropping in" at your own or somebody else's house; and a homonym for "holding" something in your hand. So the same word is used for actions involved with the ear, ghost, house, and object. Which is to say, we hear things as if we are possessed by a ghost, then we hold something in our hands and let go of it as we enter then exit somebody's house. While I was writing these poems, I was probably possessed by a ghost, listening to death, then I held death in my hand and entered the house of death. In Berlin, the angels in *Wings of Desire* do the "hearing," and in Seoul, it's the ears within poetry.

DMC: *You mention the Sewol Ferry incident of April 2014. And in the poem "Autopsy—Day Twenty-Four" you write about someone who was tortured after the May 1980 Gwangju Uprising. Do all the poems in the collection allude to specific tragic and unjust historical events?*

KH: I specifically write about the Sewol Ferry incident in "I Want to Go to the Island—Day Twenty," and "Autopsy" is about someone who had survived torture in Gwangju, then later, due to the trauma he suffered, becomes violent against his family members and eventually commits suicide. However, I never name the ferry or name the democratic uprising that took place in Gwangju in my poems. Poetry is a place in which names are never called out. It's a place where names are erased. Only I know that the poems are based on those fatal events. (In another recent book of mine, I wrote many poems that are about specific historical incidents.) I once fainted on the subway platform after feeling very dizzy. When I woke up, I discovered some people had carried me and laid me out on a bench. At that moment, something floated up and looked down at my fallen body, as if I were having an out-of-body experience. At first I wondered who she was, for I didn't recognize myself. People say that after such an experience, you gain a new realization about life, but what I saw was a universe filled with death and the humans submerged inside that death moving about pitifully like insects. I questioned whether my ethical practice had any value at all in such a universe of death. Since then, from that place filled with death, I began to write about certain deaths I had seen. As I received death inside poetry, I even experienced the death of language. To write poetry is to witness the names that die inside poetry. Poetry's climax is that moment when you discover the absence of everything—only a mustard-seed-like death remains. These poems began at the moment when death cut across our bodies, at the moment of power's violent act, its pus bursting, cornering us into murderous disparate events, but in the end, I have merely jotted down the rhythm, what the universe of death was spewing out, weeping inside each event. Why? Because rhythm is the face of death. Poetry awaited where "I" had been killed. I first published the poems in the collection one by one in various literary journals. As I read the published poems, each of them appeared to be craving the others the way each number in the multiplication table craves other numbers, even other rhythms. In Korea, we believe that when someone dies, the spirit of the dead journeys to an intermediate space that is neither death nor life for forty-nine days. I think that I may be still roaming about in one of the forty-nine days. But if I'm really alive, how is it that each and every day meaninglessly disappears into oblivion? After I finished all forty-nine poems, I wondered whether the spirits that are dead and yet alive have become one body or whether they're all separated inside each death, whether death is really separate and individual. Then I also came to think that all deaths become one enormous you, or other, or maybe one very small you.

DMC: *I've noticed that wings appear repeatedly in several poems in* Autobiography of Death—*they appear as butterfly wings, bat wings, and also as ribbons. Could you say something about them?*

KH: Your questions are very poetic. Korean critics don't ask such questions. They only ask gigantic questions. Once I went out to the night sea where nothing was visible, where the big ferry had sunk forty meters below the sea—the sea at dusk, filled with the wailings of the parents [who had lost their children]. The waves were high. All the humans that had existed on this Earth and the 800 million that were still alive, perhaps even the animals, were shaking their hair that had never been cut, running toward me. It was as if the solar system was spitting out Earth outside its sphere. The sea was in agony. It was painful, like giving birth to the devil's child, like being entwined in the devil's rhythm, like the pain of giving up your body to the rhythm. Really, it felt as if the ink inside a bottle as big as the Pacific Ocean was oscillating. I wept, wondering how I would ever use up all that ink, writing about all the unjust deaths, with my tiny pen as skinny as a butterfly's hind legs? I think the wings in my poems were probably my pen's metaphors. If my wings were as big as the Pacific Ocean, I could embrace the sunken ferry.

DMC: *I thought the English vowels you use in the poem "a e i o u—Day Twenty-Seven" acted as an alphabet of death. I thought the same for the hiccups in "Hiccups—Day Thirty-One"—the vowels and hiccups are the language and grammar of death you invent.*

KH: Women's language is a language of death. The body of a woman poet is a form of text. But it's a text of the deaf, mute, and blind. That's because the mother-tongue sits on men's tongue. Listen to the body's speech—you hear the hiccups, coughs, phlegm bubbling up. It may be that women's or death's song is sung only in vowels, without the consonants. They say the name of Father, God, is made only of consonants, but the language of women, death, is made up of sounds that come before or after language. The sounds of vowels can be made with lungs, diaphragm, kidneys, anus, genitals, and heart. Vowels are connected to the holes of the body. Women's body, the body of death, interacts with other bodies, endlessly changing and becoming. It does not objectify other bodies; instead, it wants to mix with them. It wants to multiply, longs for *assemblage*. At the place where the body becomes anonymous, disenfranchised, and expelled, is where the language of death, women's language, is born—language that grapples with the language of anonymity, negativity, non-gender specific language. The kind of writing that has definite subjects and objects, that depicts its objects in detail, objectifying them, then adding grandiose aphorisms to them is, of course, masculine writing that has been preserved in Korea by History. But the feminine writing of death begins from a place of emptiness/nothingness, a place that's full with the presence of absence. In that place, there are sounds that are considered embarrassing to the world of meaning, but not at all to the world of body (sound). In the end, what the poems in this collection want to reach is sound.

DMC: *I'm remembering what you said in our first interview back in 2001—how your poetry was perceived to be apolitical because you mostly wrote about cooking during the dictatorship of the 1980s: "What I wrote mostly about was cooking, and my ingredient was death." Your cooking recurs in all of your books that I've translated the past decade and a half, and I came to notice it again in this collection, particularly in "Dinner Menu—Day Twenty-Nine." Why is death your primary ingredient?*

KH: I cook in my kitchen daily. I'm someone who turns something alive into something dead, then eats it; I also feed what I cook to others. Wouldn't it be wonderful if I could cook with raindrops, wind, or clouds like my country's male, lyric poets? I wonder how many chickens I have eaten during my lifetime. I'm sure what I've eaten can't fit into a single dump truck. I always find myself cupping my hands before something that will die in front of me and become part of my body. However, in my poems, it's death that's doing the cooking. Empty cooking—emptiness cooks the empty. Like the mother image of Gaia—who raises all things as if they are her children in order to feed the living. Who were the children of Gaia anyway? I'm certain that they were her own body called by different names. We ultimately eat and drink our mother, consuming her endlessly. We fry up our dead mother's fingers and eat them. As I was writing, I came to realize that my daily cooking—making something alive into something dead—was the cooking of death. I cook death daily, repeatedly, in order to feed death. Otherwise, how is it that I could be hungry every day? I think this is why I'm the happiest when I can have a meal that I didn't cook.

DMC: *Women appear frequently throughout* Autobiography of Death—*they appear as mothers, daughters, and even as dolls. And I noticed this morning while I was translating "Hiccups" that it was like a fairy tale—it's about a stepmother and stepdaughter. As you know, I've been a stepmom for a while now, and I've grown to have much fondness and empathy for so-called evil stepmothers. How did all these women, particularly stepmothers, become part of your vocabulary of death?*

KH: During pregnancy, a mother and her child are interconnected; they are, in a sense, conceived together. You can't distinguish the two. But when it's time for the mother and child to become separate, the child bids farewell and enters the world filled with the death of her mother inside her. As children we all have this origin, the death of the mother inside us. Have you seen mothers embracing their dead children, crying like

Mary? The mother who has her dead child in her arms is really embracing her own death. At that moment, she's alive but dead with her child self. Have you seen Korean mothers with yellow ribbons on their chests, marching and demanding truth, demanding an investigation of the Sewol Ferry tragedy? At the memorial altar, I looked at each photograph of the fine-looking boys and girls. How do you think these children felt when they returned home from their school field trip to see that they were being placed into coffins by their parents? At the altar, I offered flowers to the children and decided to become their scribe. As a living person, I decided to become a stepmom to these children.

DMC: Autobiography *feels like a journey to me, like the journey of Princess Abandoned you write about in your groundbreaking book of feminist literary criticism,* To Write as a Woman: Lover, Patient, Poet, and You *(2002).*

KH: I published these forty-nine poems as a collection of poems, but they can be seen as a single poem. A princess named *Paridegi* [The Abandoned] is one of the famous figures in Korean mythology; at the end of her life, she becomes a boatwoman who crosses the river of the afterlife. Every day, she transfers the dead from this world to the next. She journeys endlessly into the border, the space between life and afterlife. I think the conversation inside a genre called poetry is different from the ones in our everyday life—the conversation takes place in a world where you and I don't exist, but it's a place that looks very similar to our world—perhaps a familiar-looking hallway—and that space is where Princess Abandoned, who is neither dead nor alive, makes her appearance. When we go on a journey, we usually return to the place we've left, don't we? Poetry also goes on a journey, circling once around death. As I've said in *To Write as a Woman,* Princess Abandoned repeatedly journeys to the same place, transporting death. She travels to death, then returns in order to deliver death once again. Each poem in *Autobiography* also journeys, one by one, to its own absence, then returns.

DMC: *I've noticed that the poems in* Autobiography *are relatively short compared to many of the longer prose poems in your previous books. What brought about this change?*

KH: The hours of "you" in *Autobiography* are the dreams dreamt by my death. These poems can be said to be the poems that have discovered how to deconstruct those dreams. I realized that the poetic persona of *Autobiography* has discovered the motion that travels past the substance of death, reaching a certain structure of life. Within the process of writing these poems, I came to think that death and life are of one pattern, a single repetitive form. I tried to create a faint architecture of a particular moment, which doesn't get entangled in the content of death. The incessant energy of the poetic persona, intensifying the faint architecture, became the power that pulled the poems along. Instead of boring through the content and soaring up, I dreamt of a multidimensional map that weeps in hiding. Why? Because that is what the death I was writing about looked like. And the rhythm was inherently present like death's cycle of inhalation and exhalation. The rhythm of poems proceeded while the poetic persona frantically tried to shed the music (death) that was living off of it. Rhythm was not a method of existence, but a method of lack, living inside death.

DMC: *Why the relentless use of "you" in* Autobiography?

KH: Which individual narrates my death? Can I call my death "I"? As I began to speak through my death, my death became "you." My death made the I into "not I." As I've mentioned before, poetry awaits where "I" is killed. I came to think that the you in *Autobiography* was not I or you or he/she. That is to say, the you (death) lacked any person-narrator. I kept wondering which person-narrator death might be. I thought that perhaps it was a sixth- or seventh-person narrator. The "you" in *Autobiography* is neither I, you, nor she—it's "my death." I couldn't have heard the sound of death without killing the I. The I endlessly sought after "you" through my language and death, and in order for my sensations to enter the world of poetry where "you" resides, it had to charm, declare my death, and confess its love for "you." Love is an abnormal connection between the I and you. I want to die inside you—that's love. That's why the only ethical practice of poetry is to practice the death of "I"—to fit perfectly with your body and soul. Ultimately, the I that has the eyes, nose, and mouth of death wants to become you.

DMC: *To me the last poem of the book "Face of Rhythm" is definitely a follow-up poem to* Autobiography. *I know we discussed whether to include it in this book or not. I get mentally exhausted toward the end of a translation project and can't think clearly. I'm thankful to our editor, Jeffrey Yang, for giving me a gentle push. As soon as I started translating the poem, I totally fell for it and realized that "Face" is what* Autobiography *would see if it looked itself in the mirror. So why rhythm?*

KH: I was very sick. I had severe headaches. It felt as if someone was chopping wood inside my head, and it went on for a long time. I went to several hospitals and had to take a semester off from teaching. Every morning, I wished I could perish from the pain. Then I happened to come across somebody's writing. He suffered from excruciating back pain, so he began meditating, and within a month his immense pain turned into a small, pleasurable feeling. So I began meditating too, and as soon as I closed my eyes and stayed still, a poem surfaced automatically. Pain is physical and rhythmic, whereas anguish is mental and melodic. My pain had no meaning. The only thing that lived in that meaningless space was rhythm. Rhythm is bodiless; it exists alone like the planetary orbits that keep the stars of the universe in motion, allowing us to be born then ruthlessly discarding us. The pains that came to me were mere pains sent by the gigantic rhythm, then forgotten by it. The pain was like the drumming princess of the ancient Korean Nakrang Kingdom of 2,500 years ago, or the ruling queen who sent a rhythm torturer to annihilate me. Inside a small room in South Korea, my body was writhing under the occupation of the gigantic rhythm. Eventually I realized that I needed to look directly into the face of rhythm that turns the wheel of time, the rhythm that, moreover, doesn't exist. And I thought to myself that I needed to excavate the faceless face with language, excavate the face with the rhythm embodied in language. I came to think fervently more than ever that someone involved in such idle labor is a poet.

Translator's Note

On December 3, 2016, Kim Hyesoon, her artist daughter, Fi Jae Lee, and I met at the sixth weekly candlelight protest in downtown Seoul at Gwanghwamun Square. We each carried a lit candle in a cup and a sign that read "Park Geun-hye Step Down." We sat down for a while in awe of the waves of lights and sheer number of protesters parading through the square. The surviving family members of the high school students who had drowned in the 2014 Sewol ferry disaster led the march to the gate of the president's executive office, to continue their demand for an investigation of the disaster. Kim Hyesoon turned to me and said that she hadn't been out in the streets to protest since the dictatorship of the 1980s. And it was my first protest in Seoul. I was just a child when my family left South Korea because of the dictatorship. That night, a record number 2.3 million people hit the streets nation-wide and demanded an end to Park's presidency and her corrupt, conservative administration. After the nineteenth rally, South Korea's constitutional court upheld the impeachment of President Park, the daughter of Park Chung Hee, who had enforced nearly two decades of US-backed dictatorship from 1961 to 1979.

Each of the forty-nine poems in *Autobiography of Death* represents one of the forty-nine days during which the spirit roams about after death, before it enters the cycle of reincarnation. The book concludes with a separate poem, "Face of Rhythm." When Kim Hyesoon sent me these poems, she said that she had no choice but to write them because of all the unjust deaths that have occurred in South Korea. She was referring to the recent tragic event in which 250 high school students drowned when a private passenger ferry heading to Jeju Island had capsized. Many believe neoliberal deregulation and privatization that led to safety violations played a crucial role in the sinking of the ship, including the state's dismal failure to rescue the passengers. The most recent findings have revealed that the ferry, which was carrying 1,228 tons above the legal limit, was also carrying 410 tons of iron that were meant to be used for the ongoing construction of the new naval base on the island. The base, which now hosts US and South Korean warships as well as cruise liners, has been contested by activists and residents for the past decade. Kim was also referring to the many deaths caused by the recent dictatorships, including the brutal military suppression of the pro-democratic May 1980 Uprising in the city of Gwangju. Kim says about her collection, "When one writes poetry in a country of so many deaths, it's inevitable that the voice that emerges is the voice of someone who is preoccupied with death. I was very, very sick while writing these poems. Death was in front and in back of my head, it was inside my head.... That tree doesn't know me. That rock doesn't know me. That person doesn't know me. You don't know me. I also don't know me. I wanted to die before I died."

> It's midnight and you're bored. You can't fall asleep.
> You go out on the deck. The vast sky and ocean are a black mirror. It
>   wavers.
> You think about the sleeping fish inside the black mirror.
> You think about the gluttony of the vast mirror that leaves nothing
>   behind, not even a single shadow.
> You ponder, What if starting tomorrow the days without sunrise
>   continue?
> Then we'd be inside this black mirror 24 hours a day, and who'd dip a
>   pen into the mirrorwater to write about us?
> Why is there so much ink for writing?

I believe *Autobiography of Death* is one of Kim's most important and compelling works to date. It not only gives voice to those unjustly killed during Korea's violent contemporary history, but it also unveils what Kim refers to as "the structure of death, that we remain living in." An aspect of this structure is the neocolonial and neoliberal order that has shaped Korea's history since the US intervention at the end of World War II. *Autobiography* comes after her two acclaimed long poems "Manhole Humanity" and "I'm OK, I'm Pig!," both of which also address political and military atrocities. *Autobiography* is at once an autotestimony and an autoceremony that reenacts trauma and narrates our historical death—how we have died and how we remain living within the structure of death. *Autobiography* is a sea of mirrors, hence the death we see reflected in it is the plural "you." It can only speak as a multitude. Its body beaten, bombed, buried many times over by history can only speak in multitude:

> Above you
> Below you
> Next to you
> Beneath you
> Beside you
> Beyond you
> Behind you
> Inside you

Kim Hyesoon debuted her poems in 1979, the year General Chun Doo Hwan led a coup and came into power right after Park Chung Hee was assassinated by his own intelligence officer. Kim, along with another renowned feminist poet, Ch'oe Sŭng-ja, were the first female poets to be published in South Korea's prominent literary journal *Literature and Intellect*, which took the lead in literary opposition to authoritarian rule. Kim worked as an editor then, and frequently had to go to city hall to submit each manuscript to the military censors for review. The first time I met Kim, in 2001, she told me that a play by the renowned playwright Lee Kang-Baek, whom she later married, was returned to her totally redacted except for the title and author's name. She said she wept profusely as she watched the actors perform the entire play without speaking. Then once when she was editing a biography of a pioneer feminist, she was taken to the police station. The police officer demanded the contact information of the translator of the book and slapped her seven times. Kim tells me that this experience of hers does not merit mentioning, for she was not victimized, not like those who were killed and tortured in unspeakable ways during the eras of Park and Chun. But I still think of Kim as a survivor like the way I think of my parents as survivors of the Korean War (1950–53) during which over four million, mostly civilians, were killed. About 250,000 pounds of napalm were dropped per day by the US forces. How does anyone survive such a rain of napalm? How does anyone survive unrelenting beatings? How does anyone remain living in such a structure of death?

From the late 1990s, after the establishment of civilian rule, Kim began to receive critical recognition through numerous literary awards. Her influence on the younger generation of writers, particularly women, in Korea's highly patriarchal culture is far-reaching. Kim observes that younger women poets are "developing a terrain of poetry that is combative, visceral, subversive, inventive, and ontologically feminine." As Kim often mentions when asked about her poetics, she says that she had no role models or mother tongue because Korean women's literary conventions had always been prescribed by men. However, women were free to express and explore their identities within the oral tradition of Korean shamanism. It was the only zone in which women, as performers of rites, songs, and storytelling, were not subservient to men. Kim's poetry and poetics tap into the traditional shamanistic zone, the zone women were expelled to, the zone where Princess Abandoned [*Paridegi*], a prominent female figure in shaman narratives, was left to die for being the seventh girl to be born in a row. The zone of the unwanted. This is also where the expendable, the fall-out, the collateral damage, the refugees, the exiles of the neocolonial and neoliberal wars go to. To the sea of ink. Military ink. Expelled, abandoned, and left alone to live or rot. The new tongue Kim invents, based on the long tradition of poetics and politics of expulsion, can be called expelled tongue. *Autobiography*, its multitude of death, its multitude of you, speaks expelled tongue. As an expelled child, I also speak it and translate it. I refuse to rot. For a child-translator, translation is an act of autogeography.

> Today, Mommy cooks pan-fried hair
> Yesterday, Mommy cooked braised thighs
> Tomorrow, Mommy will cook sweet and sour fingers

All of our fingers are stained by the ink of atrocities. What Ngũgĩ wa Thiong'o calls for in his 1983 essay "Writing for Peace" in *Barrel of a Pen* is more relevant than ever: "The European writer has a special responsibility. He must expose to his European audience the naked reality of the relationship between Europe and the third world.... But the responsibility also belongs to the writer from the third world. From Kenya to South Korea to South America the third world is ringed round by US nuclear and conventional military bases.... The third world writer must be on the side of the struggles of those sat upon." The same is true for the American writer of the US whose country is the leading political and economic perpetrator and producer of military ink. Kim Hyesoon's pen is a winged insect, a butterfly's hind legs: "It felt as if the ink inside a bottle as big as the Pacific Ocean was oscillating. I wept thinking how am I going to use up all that ink, writing about all the unjust deaths, with my tiny pen as skinny as a butterfly's hind legs." Within what Kim calls "a faint architecture," a form that resists the "content of death," the structure of death, everything must be winged, ribboned, tiny, or skinny to create a surface tension, to repel the ink.

> The wind that gently ties thin streaks of rain into moist ribbons and
>   pins them to your nipples has arrived
>
> ~
>
> Your wings flutter like ripples on the water
> Now are you liberated from yourself?
>
> ~
>
> You naked angel,
> you days of the day,
> with wings piddlier than a housefly's
>
> ~

Finally your first black wings flap when your body is ripped apart

But the blue hen's tiny feet are buried inside each page
Whenever you turn the page its huge wings flutter!

Eyelids fluttered like moths trying to unfold their wings and
Bodies panted under the eyelids and

A child-translator's special responsibility lies with remaining small, keeping her ink-stained fingers nimble enough to trigger a butterfly's dainty legs. Autogeography is an act of autotranslation.

§

The translation of *Autobiography of Death* was supported by a generous grant from the Literature Translation Institute of Korea (LTI-Korea). And an LTI translation residency made it possible for me to interview Kim Hyesoon in Seoul in 2016.

Thank you to the editors of the journals in which some of the poems have previously appeared: *Arkansas International, Aster(ix): Kitchen Table Translation, Columbia Journal, Cordite, Denver Quarterly, Dusie, Los Angeles Review of Books, Matter, Modern Poetry in Translation, Petra, The Poetry Review, Two Lines, Tupelo, Volta, Wave Paper,* and *Yalobusha Review.*

My deep gratitude to Deborah Woodard for reading all my drafts. To Johannes Göransson and Joyelle McSweeney of Action Books for their enduring support. To Fi Jae Lee for her incredible drawings inspired by ancient Korean Buddhist drawing technique with brush and ink. To Jeffrey Yang for his brilliant editorial insights. And to everyone at New Directions for providing a welcoming home for Kim Hyesoon's poetry.

—*Don Mee Choi*
December 5,
2016, Seoul